Head in

A Maladaptive Daydreamer's Poems

Robyn Keetley

/ BookLeaf
Publishing

Head in the Clouds - A Maladaptive
Daydreamer's Poems © 2023 Robyn
Keetley

All rights reserved.

Robyn Keetley asserts the moral right to be
identified as author of this work.

Presentation by *BookLeaf Publishing*

Web: www.bookleafpub.com

E-mail: info@bookleafpub.com

ISBN: 9789357441230

First edition 2023

For all daydreamers and their imaginary friends.

The Silent House

Silence has a hold on this house.
Thick hands choke the sound from its structure.
Sucking in my screams till they are barren
echoes of a forgotten life.

Can they hear me? Can they see me? She asks.
But no sound escapes her lips.
I pause.
He walks straight through her, dispersing her
questions till they drip down the walls and seep
through the floorboards.
Forgotten.

The story repeats.
She returns in my memory but her reflection
eludes my mirror.
Stare too long and you'll fall into the looking
glass, she warns.
I stare.

The silence has been replaced by music.
I shed this skin and I can dance again.
I shatter the mirror and will fragile shards, cut
all ties to my old life.
No one resides in that quiet house now.
The silence lingers on.

My Unfortunate Muse

I don't know,
If I am truly,
All here,
All the time.

The other me reveals herself,
In the cover of my shadow.

Her presence is a cruel reminder.
Of all I have lost.
All I will lose.
Chances not taken.
My unfortunate muse.

The Oracle

Pythia's prophecy,
One of pity.
No lies or pretty tales,
From the oracle of Delphi.

The priestess summons me,
I approach quietly;
To hear the truth she tells.

"Bloodlines lie in generational silence,
Burning effigies to familial violence.
Kindred cult, oppressing the young,
Santa Sangre, the end has begun"

The candles all burnt,
The day nearly done.
Another year suffering around this wretched sun.

Alone

They never ask me
Where I go... alone.

I put on my headphones
And pick up my phone.

I pace the floor and fly away.
For better days, I hope and pray.

I recede back, to the back of my mind.
Eager to see, what I will find.

Today I'm a poet, tomorrow a spy.
Sometimes I laugh, sometimes I cry.

These old dreams make steadfast friends.
And so I hope the dream never ends.

My Unwritten Story

I think the chapter on happiness
has been ripped from my book.
Another sad story has filled these
blank pages again.

To blotchy. Too big.
Ink spilled across the desk.

I wish your pen would entwine with mine.
Blue and black to blot out the black and blue.

We only remember how things end. I hope my
ending is happy.

But my fears are scribbled in the margins; of
being a scratched, unloved hardcover.
Abandoned on a high shelf.
Whilst someone else lives my soft paperback
life.

Pause for Applause

The heavy curtain lifts to reveal the players on the stage.
Speaking every word I've written on the page.

The don't fumble, they don't stutter. Barely uttering a mutter.
Wide eyes, beating hearts. We wait until the music starts.

Their terror is like good art and I just want to stare. No one is aware, what truly happens here.

The play ends and we go from the top.
Just because we're finished doesn't mean we stop.

The power to change the outcome and yet I never do. Perhaps I revel in the misery and sadness too.

The curtain falls, I take my bow. I'm waiting for the applause now.

My finest work to an audience of one. A lone viewer with a smoking gun.

The single watcher in a single seat. She, I hope
you never meet.

But she is me and I am her.
The separation twists and blurs.
I am her when we awake.
She is me before day break.

Just because it's not happening,
Doesn't mean it isn't feel.
For in these dreams,
I still hurt,
I still bleed,
I still feel.

A Forgotten Religion

Dead choirs can't sing.
Broken hearts can't love.

These crumbling ruins were built on cursed
foundations.

Bewitched, I still stumbled up the altar steps.
My lambs have all been sacrificed.
I can still feel the sharp sting of your knife in my
back.
Perhaps the holy water will purify the wound or
candle flames will burn my nerves to numbness.

I've never been a believer of grand ideals or
gods.
Only my dreams are real to me now.

I asked the Universe for a sign and she knocked
the breath from my lungs.
A hard hit of reality.

She handed me a map and told me to escape.
But no one can penetrate, St Peter's Gate.

The map was blank but I journeyed on. Across the impassable bridge to my mind's fortress.

Maybe one day someone will be transported here. And this lonely land will be for two.

Alien

I think I might be an alien.
Sent to study humankind.
But most of the time,
I feel I'm losing my mind.

I live among you, as one of you.
But deep down I know I don't belong.
I see your enquiring stares, the silences that go
on… for just a bit a too long.

You all seem connected in ways that I'm not.
Maybe I am human, one who has forgot.

Forever relegated to the invisible divide.
So why does it look so superficial from the
inside.

None of you seem happy. None of you content.
Yet I'm the one who's sorry, the one who has to
repent.

I wish you could come to my planet one day.
And feel as odd as I do.
But for now I remain here, I suppose it'll have to
do.

Until my kind come searching and take me to
the ship.
Back to my home planet, where I'll finally fit.

My Invisible Friend

My lonely eyes peer through the curtain.
My ear pressed against the glass.
Feet bleeding from my long pilgrimage.
How long will my penance last?

Your face only exists in my memory.
Your voice a mere whisper on the wind.
Never quiet when I'm on my own.
You're never far, my invisible friend.

The Wonder

Although I am a finite being with an infinite
soul,
Do my dreams live past this disposable form?
Will someone assume the mantle when I'm dead
and gone?
Will someone shed their skin when I pass the
baton?

I wonder if the dream would remain the same,
Or will it mould around someone new?
Twisting like vines, around their weak mind.
Until the dream is new and refined.

Assigned roles, recast.
Old stories, surpassed.

Another can't be trusted as the caretaker of my
dreams.
They would pull the story and characters apart at
the seams.

I keep the dream together so it doesn't fall apart.
I hope my dreams die with me, tucked away in
my faltering heart.

Perhaps my dreams will travel with me,
wherever I go next.
And despite these years..
The blood...the tears.
There is no great climax.

The Absurd

I embrace the absurd in all it's wild, illogical
glory.
My dreams are fantastical, there is no meaning
to the story.

I am the Universe experiencing itself.
How can they make sense?
How can I bottle life's great meaning?
How do I condense?

My dreams are the proverbial rock, pushed by
Sisyphus up the hill.
I don't know why I repeat the dream, but I know
each day I will.

When life overwhelms you and becomes to
much to bear.
Remember the words of Camus -
'I like people who dream. They are here and
elsewhere'

In Somnis Veritas

In dreams there is truth,
Ugly and malformed.
A monster tucked away in youth,
Abandoned and deformed.

The mind reveals your thoughts and feelings,
Naked and exposed.
As you stare up at your ceiling,
Willing your eyes to close.

Dreams are escape from reality,
but hiding under your bed.
Slashing, clawing, sad and beastly,
Is the monster in your head.

You may aspire to live in a dream, to escape this
plane and ascend.
But you can't outrun your life, it seems, it'll
catch you in the end.

My Nightmare

Light dies in the dark realm.
The shadows come alive.
Jump off the walls,
Collecting souls,
Devouring to thrive.

My nightmares have a heartbeat,
Feasting on my fears.
A mass consuming appetite,
Punch-drunk on my tears.

Tearing memories from the bone,
Tender and profound.
Blood gushing from the wound,
Screams fading in the background.

Nightmares are where we hide,
Our ugly, moulding shame.
Dreams are where we come alive,
A passionate burning flame.

Here, There

Here, I am brilliant.
There, I am dull.
Here, is silent.
There, an earful.

Here, is control.
There, is chaos.
Here, is abundance.
There, is great loss.

Here, is where I run.
There, is where I lie.
Here, is where I laugh.
There, is where I cry.

Here, is lonely but free.
There, is busy and loud.
Here, a brilliant rainbow.
There, a grey storm cloud.

Shattered

Sharp words cut like glass,
Cutting holes, finding homes.
Sitting on my mind for days,
Digging deep into my bones.

Shattering through vertebrae,
Paralysed by pain.
Written in my epitaph,
Another black ink stain.

My mind translates the message,
To something far more kinder.
Insults become compliments,
Happiness, I will find her.

Untangling wired barbs,
Wrapped around my heart.
A dictionary of dreams,
To block the cruel remarks.

In dreams I decide the words,
Whispered, spoken and said.
So move in close and listen hard,
Believe kind words instead.

Patterns

Patterns can present themselves in Nature,
Space, in Time.
Children fall from half the trees they're brave
enough to climb.

Leaves will die in Winter then return to us in
Spring.
And bees will drop for every person that they
choose to sting.

Tomorrow you'll be happy even if today you're
sad.
Follow the pattern and you'll see not every day is
bad.

You've lived through every hardship, you've ever
had to face.
And if the end seems out of reach,
Remember:
It's a marathon, not a race.

Adrift

Two black holes colliding.
Fantasy and reality.
The unescapable force dragging me in.
All the power of the stars can't compete with my
mind, when the daydream begins.

There's no Big Bang to signal the beginning, just
symphony and song.
I pace away till I float to space,
I won't be gone for long.

I dance between the galaxies and from a distance
I can see.
The faces of forgotten friends come back to
welcome me.

So when I am adrift in space,
untethered and unbound.
I rely on you to pull me back and anchor me to
the ground.

The Authors

The Bronte's had Angria and Gondal,
before their writing success.
Conflict, romance and adventure,
The Rulers of Verdopolis.

Before Lewis put his pen to page,
Narnia was called Boxen.
Still a fantastical world of magic,
created with his brother Warren.

Tolkein's dreams started in childhood,
but drew heavily from the Great War.
Elves, Orcs, Hobbits and Men,
Expressing trauma felt before.

These wondrous paracosms,
As they were commonly named.
Existed long before,
These great authors achieved fame.

So if you feel you are wasting your life,
On things unreal, untrue.
Just remember your favourite writers,
felt the same way too.

The Dream

When reality blends with imaginary.
When you invent new worlds for yourself.
When you suffer some great tragedy.
And prefer to live stories on the bookshelf.

When the movies are more appealing,
Then your current life at home.
When you can't express your feelings.
When you always feel alone.

When the reality of your situation,
Overwhelms you with fear and dread.
When you have no solid foundation,
to rest your wear head.

When this world isn't everything,
you imagine in your dreams.
Float away on bed springs,
Transported by moonbeams.

The Temptation

Hearts are fickle and corruptible,
they influence what we do.
The devil can always find hard work,
for idle minds too.

Hallucinations so vivid and inviting,
I almost give up, give in.
Lost in some hypnotic state,
Embrace the wretch within.

I know it's an illusion,
A castle on the cloud.
But can you blame me for escaping,
When life becomes too loud.

Head in the Clouds

A singular raincloud, a locked door and master
key.
Feels just like smoke, wrapping itself around
me.

It covers my head and shields my eyes.
My vision filled with vivid lightning and blue
skies.

And just when I feel I'm floating away...
Someone tugs my hand and begs me to stay.

The cloud disappears...to return another day.

Milton Keynes UK
Ingram Content Group UK Ltd.
UKHW050027250324
439966UK00014BA/972

9 789357 441230